THE STORY OF EMMA LAZARUS

LIBERTY'S
Voice

Erica Silverman * ILLUSTRATED BY *Stacey Schuett*

Dutton Children's Books *An imprint of Penguin Group (USA) Inc.*

In memory of my immigrant grandparents—
Pearl & Isidore, Rose & Jacob—and to the immigrants of today . . . —E.S.

In memory of my great-grandparents, who made the journey —S.S.

DUTTON CHILDREN'S BOOKS
A division of Penguin Young Readers Group

Published by the Penguin Group
Penguin Group (USA) Inc., 375 Hudson Street, New York, New York 10014, U.S.A.
Penguin Group (Canada), 90 Eglinton Avenue East, Suite 700, Toronto, Ontario M4P 2Y3, Canada (a division of Pearson Penguin Canada Inc.)
Penguin Books Ltd, 80 Strand, London WC2R 0RL, England • Penguin Ireland, 25 St Stephen's Green, Dublin 2, Ireland (a division of Penguin Books Ltd)
Penguin Group (Australia), 250 Camberwell Road, Camberwell, Victoria 3124, Australia (a division of Pearson Australia Group Pty Ltd) • Penguin Books
India Pvt Ltd, 11 Community Centre, Panchsheel Park, New Delhi - 110 017, India • Penguin Group (NZ), 67 Apollo Drive, Rosedale, North Shore 0632,
New Zealand (a division of Pearson New Zealand Ltd) • Penguin Books (South Africa) (Pty) Ltd, 24 Sturdee Avenue, Rosebank, Johannesburg 2196,
South Africa • Penguin Books Ltd, Registered Offices: 80 Strand, London WC2R 0RL, England

Library of Congress Cataloging-in-Publication Data
Silverman, Erica.
Liberty's voice: the story of Emma Lazarus/by Erica Silverman ;
illustrated by Stacey Schuett.—1st ed.   p. cm.
Includes bibliographical references.
ISBN 978-0-525-47859-1
1. Lazarus, Emma, 1849–1887—Juvenile literature. 2. Poets, American—19th century—Biography—Juvenile literature.
3. Women social reformers—United States—Biography—Juvenile literature. I. Schuett, Stacey, ill.
II. Title. III. Title: story of Emma Lazarus.
PS2234.S55 2011
811'.4—dc22   [B]   2010013186

Published in the United States by Dutton Children's Books, • a division of Penguin Young Readers Group
345 Hudson Street, New York, New York 10014 • www.penguin.com/youngreaders

Designed by Abby Kuperstock

Manufactured in China • First Edition
1 3 5 7 9 10 8 6 4 2

Emma Lazarus loved to learn. She had a passion for words and a hunger for knowledge. This passion would one day make her the voice of Liberty.

But back in 1849, when Emma was born, people believed learning was not ladylike and that girls who used their brains too much would become ill. Fortunately, Emma's father did not agree. And because Moses Lazarus was a well-to-do sugar refiner, he brought tutors into his home for Emma and her siblings.

Growing up in New York's bustling Union Square, Emma learned from her books as well as from the world around her.

Most of all, from the time she was very young, Emma loved poetry. Poets gave words such power! How, she wondered, could she ever learn to write like that?

Then one day, while reading a book by the popular author Ralph Waldo Emerson, she came upon some words that seemed to speak directly to her, words that spoke of "listening to the whisper of the voice within . . ."

She listened . . . and from somewhere deep within, words grew and images took shape.

Emma began to write.

Emma found inspiration everywhere. She filled up one notebook after another with poetry. She wrote of her grief at the death of a friend, the heroism of a Civil War general, and the beautiful Greek goddess Aphrodite, rising from the ocean.

She carried her notebook wherever she went. She took it to the family's summerhouse in Newport, Rhode Island.

While her brother and five sisters ran and played, she wrote and rewrote.

She had her notebook with her when she visited the one-hundred-year-old synagogue built by Spanish and Portuguese Jews who had come seeking safety and freedom. Refusing to betray their religion, they had left their homelands, not knowing where they would go or how they would survive. Among them was Emma's many-times-great-grandfather.

Emma stood in the shadowy light of the old prayer house and imagined how they must have felt. She listened to a voice, a whisper, within. Words grew. Images took shape. She wrote:

What prayers were in this temple offered up,
Wrung from sad hearts that knew no joy on earth,
By these lone exiles of a thousand years,
From the fair sunrise land that gave them birth!

Emma's notebook filled up with poems, but . . . were they any good? Nervously, she showed them to her father.

Moses Lazarus was pleased—his daughter had talent. To encourage her, he had a small book of her work printed. *Poems and translations by Emma Lazarus, written between the ages of Fourteen and Seventeen*, was distributed to family and friends.

The family was proud—their Emma was a poet!

Editors at a publishing company agreed. The following year, they published her book for a wider audience. Poetry continued to spill from Emma's pen.

One winter evening, Emma went with her parents to a dinner party. Guiding her across the room toward a white-haired gentleman with wise, penetrating eyes, her father announced, "Emma, I want to introduce you to Mr. Ralph Waldo Emerson."

The famous author—the one whose book had taught her to listen within—greeted her politely. Emma soon found herself speaking comfortably with Mr. Emerson. Amazingly, he listened to her, a girl of nineteen, with genuine interest. She told him she had a published volume of poems.

"I'd like to read it," he said.

Emma mailed Mr. Emerson a copy of her book. Two weeks later, she received his response.

My dear Miss Lazarus,
I have happy recollections of the conversation at Mr. Ward's, that I am glad to have them confirmed by the possession of your book and letter.

Emma flushed with happiness. Mr. Emerson liked her poems! Or . . . was he just being kind? And why hadn't he said anything critical? Emma needed him to be honest, to point out the failings in her work, so she could learn. She wrote back:

I should have been pleased if you had marked . . . passages in my poem . . . (that) you disapproved of, for I would like to correct . . . as much as is in my power . . .

Once again, she waited. Would Mr. Emerson be willing to teach her? His next letter brought the answer she hoped for:

I should like to be appointed your professor, you being required to attend the whole term. I should . . . insist on large readings and writings . . .

Emma was thrilled!

She read all the books Mr. Emerson recommended. Paying careful attention to his advice, she pushed herself hard, cutting words, writing and rewriting. One poem and then another was accepted by a magazine. Her second book was published and then her third. Mr. Emerson's young student was growing up, making a name for herself.

In addition to poetry, Emma wrote essays and book reviews. She attended museum events, plays, and concerts. In a letter to a friend she said, "I don't know when I have been . . . so interested in people, books, art, music—everything that is to be enjoyed."

Emma's writing became a regular feature of the *Century*, the most widely read magazine in the country. The editor and his wife were among her closest friends. They introduced her to a politician, William Evarts, who invited her to a mass protest rally. This event would change Emma's life and infuse her writing with new purpose.

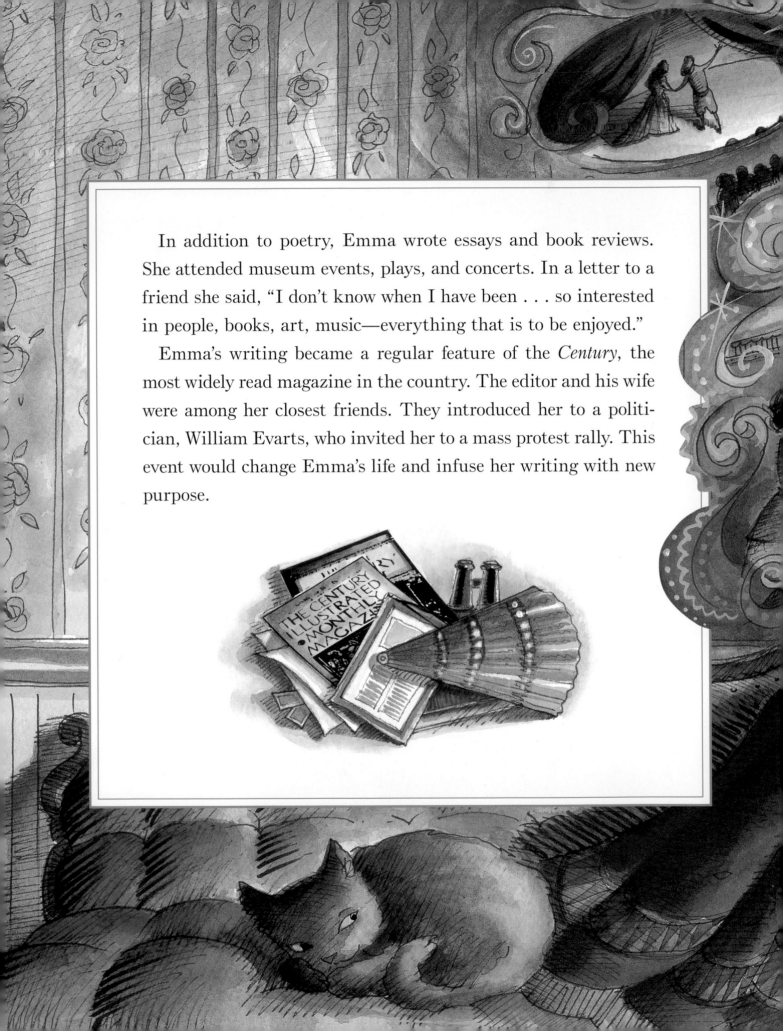

One evening, Emma entered a hall thronged with all kinds of people, speaking many different languages. Tension filled the air.

Mr. Evarts took the stage. The Jews in Russia, he announced, had recently become victims of terrible violence. He described pogroms—raging mobs roving from town to town, beating and killing Jewish men, women, and children; burning down their homes; stealing their belongings. Emma listened, shocked and sickened. She had believed that hatred and violence against Jews were things of the past; now she felt called upon to defend her people.

Emma wrote newspaper articles denouncing the pogroms.

Then she went to visit the victims of violence, Russian Jews who were pouring into New York Harbor, seeking sanctuary. She saw hundreds of refugees, hungry and scared, crammed together in four temporary tar-covered barracks on Ward's Island. There was no running water. The bread was raw and doughy and the soup had worms. Children played in piles of garbage. Outraged, Emma wrote an article exposing the frightful conditions.

She brought food and clothing, set up English classes, organized groups, raised money, met with government officials, helped to start a trade school.

But not everyone welcomed the newcomers. Some, blaming immigrants for crime, disease, and poverty, called for new laws to keep them out. Emma worked harder to change attitudes.

Suddenly her writing was fueled by anger at injustice, pride in her heritage, and hope for a better world. New poems, plays, and articles spilled from her pen at a furious pace. She wrote:

"Until we are all free, we are none of us free."

Emma decided to meet with Jewish leaders in England to talk about the Russian Jewish problem. She had since childhood dreamed of visiting England, France, and Italy, of seeing all the places she had read about in books. So, accompanied by her sister Josephine, she sailed for Europe. They traveled across England and Italy, writing enthusiastic letters home about the places they visited and the people they met.

On the return voyage, Emma's ship sailed through New York Harbor. Here she was, arriving along the same waterway as the immigrants who came carrying everything they owned, uncertain of the future, not knowing even the language of their new home. How fortunate she felt, greeted by friends and family, eager to share delightful stories of her happy adventures abroad. How important that her dear homeland continue to welcome its immigrants, that it strive to live up to its ideals of equality.

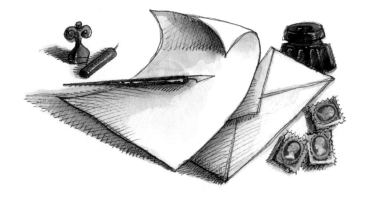

Piles of letters awaited Emma. One was from Mr. Evarts. France, he wrote her, had sent the United States a massive statue called Liberty Enlightening the World. But the statue needed a base and a base was expensive. He was chairing the Pedestal Fund Committee and holding an auction to raise funds. Would she please write a poem about the statue to donate to the event?

"I am sorry, but I can not write to order," she wrote back. "Poetry must come from the heart."

Evarts did not give up. He sent a committee member, Constance Cary Harrison, to Emma's home. Harrison pleaded with Emma.

Emma remained firm. "A poem written to order would be flat."

Harrison pressed on. "Think of that goddess standing on her pedestal down yonder in the bay and holding her torch out to those Russian refugees of yours."

Emma sighed. "The auction is next week. Even if I wanted to, I would never be able to write a poem so quickly."

But Emma was stirred by Harrison's words. She pictured the immigrants coming into New York Harbor for the first time, their eyes alighting on the statue called Liberty. In newspaper articles, it was always being compared to the Colossus of Rhodes, a famous Greek statue, male, overpowering, meant to frighten away intruders. Liberty was massive and powerful, too, but unlike the old Colossus, she seemed to be holding up her torch to light the way, to welcome the newcomers.

Emma set down a title, "The New Colossus."

Then she listened to the whisper of the voice deep within. Words grew. Images took shape.

She wrote:

Not like the brazen giant of Greek fame,
With conquering limbs astride from land to land;
Here at our sea-washed, sunset gates shall stand
A mighty woman with a torch, whose flame
Is the imprisoned lightning, and her name . . .

Emma stopped. What was the right name for her?

Emma thought about the immigrants she had met on Ward's Island. They had known so much fear and suffering. They needed to be held, welcomed, comforted. If this statue was to have a name, it should be . . .

Mother of Exiles. From her beacon-hand
Glows world-wide welcome; her mild eyes command
The air-bridged harbor that twin cities frame.

And if the statue spoke to the world, what would she say? Emma listened. And wrote . . .

"Keep ancient lands, your storied pomp!" cries she
With silent lips. "Give me your tired, your poor,
Your huddled masses yearning to breathe free,
The wretched refuse of your teeming shore.
Send these, the homeless, tempest-tost to me,
I lift my lamp beside the golden door!"

Emma set down her pen. She had done it! She had poured her hopes and dreams for the immigrants into the poem. Perhaps it would do some good.

"The New Colossus" was the only piece of writing read aloud at the auction on December 3, 1883. The poet James Russell Lowell wrote to Lazarus, saying, "I liked your sonnet about the statue. Much better than I like the statue itself . . . your sonnet gives its subject a raison d'être which it wanted before quite as much as it wanted a pedestal."

Emma never knew the importance of the poem. She died in 1887. In 1903, the poem was engraved on a plaque and attached to the base of the Statue of Liberty.

Over time, the poem and the statue came to be permanently linked. The Statue of Liberty continues to be seen as the Mother of Exiles, a beacon of hope to immigrants all over the world.

When Emma died, memorial tributes poured in from around the world. Joseph Gilder wrote, "We lament the loss to humanity of a woman of high ideals and noble enthusiasms, a courageous and chivalric fighter whose lance was raised effectively in defence of the oppressed." (*American Hebrew*, Nov. 28, 1887)

Bibliography and Further Reading

BOOKS

Cowen, Philip. *Memories of an American Jew.* New York: Arno, 1975.

Gilder, Rosamond (ed.). *Letters of Richard Watson Gilder.* Boston & New York: Houghton Mifflin, 1916.

Lazarus, Emma. *The Poems of Emma Lazarus.* 2 volumes. Boston: Houghton Mifflin and Company, 1889.

Manners, Ande. *Poor Cousins.* New York: Coward, McCann & Geoghegan, 1972.

Merriam, Eve. *Emma Lazarus: Woman with a Torch.* New York: Citadel Press, 1956.

Schappes, Morris U. *The Letters of Emma Lazarus, 1868–1885.* New York: NYPL, 1949.

Young, Bette Roth. *Emma Lazarus in Her World: Life and Letters.* New York: Jewish Publication Society, 1995.

ARTICLES

American Hebrew 9, "The Memorial Issue." December, 1887.

Cowen, Philip. "Recollections of Emma Lazarus." *American Hebrew* (July 05, 1929) 229, 240-1.

Lazarus. Emma. "The Schiff Refuge." *American Hebrew.* Oct. 27, 1882, p 125.

—. "Cruel Bigotry." *American Hebrew.* May 25, 1883, p. 14.

—. "Consolation." *American Hebrew.* May 11, 1883, p. 147.

—. "Progress and Poverty." New York *Times,* Oct. 2, 1881.

—. "The Outrages in Russia." *Century* 23, (6), Apr 1882.

Lazarus, Josephine. "Emma Lazarus." *Century* 36. October 1888.

FOR FURTHER READING

Curlee, Lynn. *Liberty.* New York: Aladdin, 2003.

Levinson, Nancy Smiler. *I Lift My Lamp: Emma Lazarus and the Statue of Liberty.* New York: Dutton Children's Books, 1986.

Maestro, Betsy & Giulio. *The Story of the Statue of Liberty.* New York: Harper, 1989.

WEBSITES

Statue of Liberty Website: http://www.statueofliberty.org

Ellis Island Website: http://www.ellisisland.org

Jewish Women's Archive: http://www.jwa.orgexhibts.wov/lazarus

Emma Lazarus Fund: http://www2.soros.org/emma/